THE ANTOINETTE MATLINS *"RIGHT-WAY"* SERIES
ON USING GEM IDENTIFICATION TOOLS

SSEF DIAMOND-TYPE SPOTTER AND BLUE DIAMOND TESTER
Made Easy

The "RIGHT-WAY" Guide to Using Gem Identification Tools

ANTOINETTE MATLINS, PG, FGA

GEMSTONE PRESS
Woodstock, Vermont

www.gemstonepress.com

D1592657

SSEF Diamond-Type Spotter and Blue Diamond Tester Made Easy:
The "RIGHT-WAY" Guide to Using Gem Identification Tools

2014 Paperback Edition, First Printing

The Library of Congress has cataloged the previous edition of *Gem Identification Made Easy*, from which this booklet is drawn, as follows:
Matlins, Antoinette Leonard.
Gem identification made easy : a hands-on guide to more confident buying & selling. —5th edition.
     pages cm
Written by Antoinette Matlins and A.C. Bonanno.
Includes bibliographical references and index.
ISBN 978-0-943763-90-3 (hc)
1. Precious stones—Identification. I. Bonanno, Antonio C. II. Title.
          QE392.M33 2013
          553.8028'7—dc23

Some of the material in *Gem Identification Made Easy* appeared originally as articles in *National Jeweler*.

SSEF Diamond-Type Spotter and Blue Diamond Tester Made Easy:
The "RIGHT-WAY" Guide to Using Gem Identification Tools
ISBN 978-0-9904152-5-1 (pbk)
ISBN 978-0-943763-99-6 (eBook)

Cover Design: Jenny Buono, Stefan Killen and Bridgett Taylor
Text Design: James F. Brisson
Illustrations: Kathleen Robinson

10   9   8   7   6   5   4   3   2   1

Manufactured in the United States of America
Published by GemStone Press
A Division of LongHill Partners, Inc.
Sunset Farm Offices, Rte. 4, P.O. Box 237
Woodstock, VT 05091
Tel: (802) 457-4000 Fax: (802) 457-4004
www.gemstonepress.com

THE SSEF DIAMOND-TYPE SPOTTER AND SSEF BLUE DIAMOND TESTER—ESSENTIAL TOOLS FOR DIAMOND BUYERS

Today, an increasing number of *synthetic colorless diamonds* are being produced. (Note: when the term "colorless" is used here, we are referring to diamonds in the D–Z category as opposed to fancy colors.) As you know, synthetic diamonds have essentially the same physical and optical properties as diamond, but they are created in factories or laboratories rather than having formed naturally within the earth. Colorless synthetics are now commercially available in a variety of sizes. There is nothing wrong with the product, and it has its place in the jewelry market, but these "new" colorless synthetics are making headlines because of the increasing number being sold as "natural" diamonds. To complicate matters further from a gemological perspective, many *naturally occurring* diamonds are also being *treated* by ever-more sophisticated HPHT techniques to *transform* them from tinted or undesirable colors into more desirable colors; HPHT-treated stones include *colorless* stones— by far the largest segment of the diamond market—as well as a variety of lovely colors. Here again, there is nothing wrong with the product itself, but with people failing to disclose the treatment and selling them as natural-color diamonds, at higher prices it is important to be able to distinguish them from one another.

Today, we also have HPHT techniques used in conjunction with other techniques, such as irradiation, to create a wider range of colors, including higher grades in colorless diamonds as well as more "fancy" colors (some much more "natural" looking in appearance).

These developments have caused tremendous fear in today's marketplace because some of the synthetic diamonds and HPHT-treated diamonds have overlapping identification features that make positive identification more difficult.

A Short History of the HPHT Process and Diamond Synthesis

About a decade ago, the technique that has come to be referred to as *HPHT* (for "high pressure/high temperature") was introduced to transform very tinted or off-color diamonds into colorless and near-colorless stones, as well as a range of fancy colors. HPHT techniques can also—albeit this is very rare—transform "brown" diamonds into extremely rare blue and pink colors, as well as *improve* the color of natural-color blue and fancy pink diamonds by removing detrimental brownish undertones and, thus, intensifying the color. The HPHT process created widespread alarm because determining for sure whether or not any diamond of fine color had been treated by HPHT requires sophisticated testing available only at major gem-testing laboratories.

Simultaneously, HPHT technology was having an impact on the feasibility of synthesizing diamonds. By the 1980s, synthetic diamonds were commercially available in various shades of "fancy" yellow, and by the 1990s, synthetic pink and blue diamonds began to enter the market. Where fancy colors are concerned, most can be identified with standard gemological testing (fluorescence, inclusions, spectroscopic examination, and so on). Furthermore, for diamonds in the rarest colors, even in very small sizes, laboratory reports usually accompany the stone. So where fancy colors were concerned, there was less anxiety about them in the trade.

Colorless synthetic diamonds posed greater technological challenges. While colorless synthetic diamonds produced by single-crystal chemical vapor deposition (CVD) entered the market over a decade ago, initial production was limited to small sizes (most under ½ carat), fairly tinted colors (J–M), and sold at high prices, so there weren't many in the marketplace. Recent technological advances have changed this. Today we find much better colors and clarities (E–F color/VS–SI clarity) and a good supply of cut and polished stones in one-carat sizes; labs are also beginning to see cut and polished colorless synthetic diamonds weighing over 2 carats.

It is easy to see why anyone buying and selling diamonds today is concerned about the challenges presented by synthetic and HPHT-treated diamonds in terms of identification since most gemologists can't afford the equipment necessary to know for sure. Thus, everyone thought they would need to send *all diamonds* to a major laboratory.

Fortunately, this is not the case. Where colorless diamonds are concerned—which account for approximately 80% of all diamond sales—*all* **synthetic** *diamonds, and all* **HPHT-treated** *diamonds are a very rare diamond type, known as* **Type II**. This distinction is of major importance because it means that with a pre-screening tool, you have the ability to know—most of the time—when the diamond you're examining is *not* a synthetic or HPHT-treated colorless/near-colorless diamond. This greatly reduces dependency on major gem-testing laboratories.

Pre-Screening Made Easy with Tools Such as the SSEF Diamond-Type Spotter

Pre-screening colorless diamonds (as well as pink and blue diamonds) to determine whether or not they are Type I or Type II is essential today. Where colorless diamonds are concerned, if it is *not* a Type II diamond, *then it cannot have been whitened by HPHT to create a colorless stone, nor can it be a colorless synthetic diamond!*

This is significant because experts estimate that only *about 2% of all diamonds are Type II*. This means that, when examining *colorless* diamonds, a simple pre-screening device will enable you to know—for sure—about 98% of the time whether or not the stone being examined is synthetic or a type that *could* have been enhanced by HPHT. (This percentage drops as size increases, but it still provides reassurance approximately 80–90% of the time, even for large diamonds.) Only in a small percentage of cases will you need to submit a colorless diamond to a major laboratory for confirmation as to whether it is a natural or treated Type II diamond, or one of the new colorless synthetic diamonds.

Thus, by pre-screening to determine whether or not a diamond is a Type I or Type II, you can reassure yourself *most of the time* about what you are buying and selling when it comes to colorless diamonds.

This is where tools such as the SSEF Diamond-Type Spotter provide an invaluable aid and greatly reduces dependency on laboratories. Only when a diamond is found to be a Type II is a major laboratory needed to know for sure.

In addition, many seek out brown-tinted diamonds today in the hope they can be transformed into much rarer, more desirable colors, and the spotter is invaluable as a tool to determine whether or not this can be done.

USING THE SSEF DIAMOND-TYPE SPOTTER TO SCREEN FOR COLORLESS SYNTHETIC DIAMONDS AND HPHT-ENHANCED DIAMONDS

The Swiss Gemmological Institute (SSEF) developed a simple tool to separate Type I from Type II diamonds. It is called the SSEF Diamond-Type Spotter, and its use greatly reduces anxiety and risk. We are going to discuss only this instrument here because it was the first instrument to distinguish between diamond types, and we are familiar with it. Today there is a similar instrument from HRD in Belgium.

In the case of *colorless* diamonds, the SSEF Diamond-Type Spotter makes it easy for *anyone* to quickly determine whether a diamond is one of the rare types that *could* be synthetic or treated. (NOTE: *all colorless synthetic diamonds produced today are Type II.*) If you discover the diamond is *not* a Type II, you do not have to worry about it being synthetic, nor worry that its color has been enhanced by HPHT. If, however, you discover the diamond *is* Type II, then you'll know you *must* send the stone to a lab to know for sure. In the case of brownish diamonds, it will tell you whether or not the color is improvable; that is, if it is a type that can be de-colorized by HPHT. In the case of *fancy-color* diamonds, the spotter has a more limited use—and we recommend that *all* fancy-color diamonds be submitted to a major lab for a current report confirming color origin—but it is a useful tool nonetheless, especially where blue diamonds are concerned.

DISTINGUISHING TYPE I DIAMONDS FROM TYPE II DIAMONDS

Since diamonds are in such high demand and represent such an important percentage of all jewelry sales, there is growing concern today about the number of "colorless" diamonds (that is, those in the D–Z category, rather than "fancy-color" diamonds) being sold without proper identification or disclosure. Of immediate concern is how to identify naturally colorless, natural diamonds from colorless *synthetic* diamonds and those that have been enhanced by HPHT methods. Fortunately, in the case of colorless synthetic diamonds and those transformed by HPHT into colorless stones, the process requires a rare diamond type, *Type IIa* (see diamond-type chart on page 9). Type IIa diamonds can also occur naturally in colorless to near-colorless grades, *but most colorless diamonds are Type Ia.* As mentioned earlier, it has been estimated by diamond producers that Type IIa diamonds represent less than 2% of *all* diamonds mined. (Note: the percentage is higher among larger diamonds with high clarity grades—over three carats—and Type II diamonds may be as high as 20% of stones over ten carats with clarity grades of VS and better.)

As mentioned earlier, distinguishing between natural and synthetic colorless diamonds, and detecting the use of HPHT methods to remove the tint to create a whiter diamond, can only be done with sophisticated testing available at major gem-testing laboratories. From a practical standpoint, however, it is not always possible to send a stone to a lab before making a buying decision, nor can anyone afford to send *every* diamond to a gem-testing lab. *However, in the case of colorless and near-colorless diamonds, it isn't necessary to send every stone to a lab, because the SSEF Diamond-Type Spotter enables you to know whether or not the diamond is a Type IIa. If it is not, no lab is needed!*

If the SSEF spotter shows you that a colorless diamond in question is *not* a Type IIa—which will be *most* of the time—then you know *it is not a synthetic* diamond and it *could not have been HPHT-treated*, so no lab is needed and you can rest assured that the stone is a natural diamond and not HPHT-enhanced. Conversely, if it *is* a Type IIa, then you will know that you *must* send the stone to a lab in order for the lab to determine whether it is a natural Type IIa diamond, a synthetic diamond, or one that has been HPHT-treated.

Note: **In cases where diamonds are accompanied by a diamond grading report issued prior to the year 2000, we recommend that it be resubmitted to a lab for confirmation. Prior to 2000, laboratories had not yet compiled sufficient data to know how to separate HPHT-treated colorless and near-colorless diamonds from the natural.**

HPHT-Treated "Fancy-Color" Diamonds

In addition to colorless diamonds, HPHT techniques can also be used to transform undesirable shades into much more desirable "fancy" colors. The fancy colors produced by HPHT currently include some of the more common colors, such as yellow to yellow-green shades, but also pink and blue shades, colors which are very rare and very costly when they occur naturally. The greatest risk occurs when considering rare fancy blue and fancy pink diamonds. Both natural-color pink and blue diamonds and those that have been HPHT-enhanced are extremely rare and costly, but HPHT-treated stones should sell for much less than the natural. In the case of *all pink and most blue diamonds,* it is essential to obtain *current* laboratory confirmation, and we recommend it for costly fancy-color diamonds, in all colors.

In the case of blue diamonds, the spotter *may* enable you to know immediately whether a diamond was HPHT-treated. In the case of blue diamonds, there are two diamond types: those containing boron (Type IIb) and those containing hydrogen (as found in some blue diamonds mined in Australia). The hydrogen type "blue" diamonds are very rare, and are typically a grayish blue or violet-blue, so they are usually not confused with those that are Type IIb. It is easy to separate them using the diamond type-spotter. With the spotter, the boron type will show the same reaction as Type IIa; the hydrogen type will show the same reaction you see for Type Ia. So, if you are checking a blue diamond using the SSEF spotter as explained below, and you do *not* get the reaction indicated below for a Type IIb diamond and the color has a definite grayish or violet hue, *then* you know the diamond is probably a natural color, hydrogen-type blue diamond. But this is the only case where we would rely on the result of the spotter when it comes to fancy-color diamonds. Also, do not forget that diamonds can be color-altered by irradiation techniques, with blue being one of the most popular irradiated colors; the color of the hydrogen-type blue diamond, however, is not produced by irradiation. A Type IIb diamond is also electrically conductive, but irradiated blue diamonds are not, so if you have the SSEF Blue Diamond Tester, or an electrical conductivity meter, it will enable you to identify Type IIb blue diamonds even without the SSEF Diamond-Type Spotter.

In the case of yellow and greenish-yellow diamonds, the spotter is *not* useful, so *all* diamonds in these hues must be sent to a lab.

If checking a brown or brownish diamond, the SSEF Diamond-Type Spotter will tell you whether or not you have a Type II, which could be improved by HPHT treatment, and the SSEF Blue Diamond Tester, or other electrical conductivity meter, will then tell you if the diamond is the rare Type IIb that will become *blue* when HPHT-treated.

We advise anyone buying any fancy-color diamond, or piece of jewelry containing fancy-color melee, to submit the stone to a major gem-testing laboratory for confirmation that they are natural and not synthetic, and whether or not the color is natural.

USING THE SSEF DIAMOND-TYPE SPOTTER

Below we will explain what the diamond-type spotter is, what it is showing, and how to use it. In addition, we will explain how HPHT methods can reveal pink and blue diamonds, or improve the purity of color in naturally pink and blue diamonds. All pink diamonds and most blue diamonds, whether they are natural-color or the result of HPHT techniques, will give the same reaction with the spotter and *must* be sent to a lab for confirmation.

What Is the SSEF Diamond-Type Spotter?

The spotter is a cylindrical, pocket-size instrument that is used in conjunction with a shortwave ultraviolet lamp. It has an opening on the top, surrounded by a ring of plasticine (silly putty), and an opening at the front. At the base of the front opening, you will notice a white coating. This special coating *fluoresces green when exposed to shortwave ultraviolet light.* If the coating fluoresces when testing a colorless, pink, or blue diamond, you'll know you have a diamond type that might be a synthetic diamond, or one that may have been HPHT-treated to create the color you are seeing. As you begin using the spotter to test diamonds, you will soon see that most of the time the diamonds are *not* a type that would indicate "synthetic" or "HPHT processing," and you'll know you don't have to worry or incur the costs of laboratory testing. In those cases where a diamond *is* a type that could be either of these, you will know you *must* send the stone to a major laboratory in order to know for sure. But since the spotter will usually indicate the diamond is not one of the rare types that might be synthetic or improvable by HPHT techniques, this simple screening test will save you lots of time, money, and needless concern.

What Is the Spotter Actually Testing?

When you test a stone with the SSEF spotter, you are actually testing the *shortwave transparency* of the stone; that is, whether or not it *transmits* shortwave radiation. There are basically four diamond "types"; some of these types transmit shortwave and others do not. The rare types that *can* be transformed by HPHT techniques to create colorless, near-colorless, pink, and blue diamonds *do transmit* shortwave, and other diamond types do *not.*

What Does the Spotter Tell You?

The spotter tells you whether the diamond is transmitting shortwave and, thus, enables you to place any diamond into one of two categories: those that *do* transmit shortwave versus those that *do not.* As you can see from the chart on pages 9–10, most diamonds belong to the category that does *not* transmit shortwave. Colorless and blue synthetic diamonds, and diamonds that can be transformed into colorless, near-colorless, pink, and blue diamonds by the HPHT process, belong to a category that *does* transmit shortwave. Therefore, by using this simple tool, you can determine whether or not the stone transmits shortwave and, thus, whether or not you need the services of a major laboratory for positive determination.

Diamond Types* and Their Response to HPHT Techniques

Type I Diamonds

Type IaA and Type IaA/B diamonds do *not* transmit shortwave ultraviolet light (they *absorb* it). Most diamonds are this type ("Cape" diamonds). There is also a very rare gray-blue to violet-blue diamond that is Type IaA. Type IaA/B stones may be HPHT-treated, but they do not produce colorless, near-colorless, pink, or blue stones.

Type Ib diamonds also do *not* transmit shortwave ultraviolet light. (These belong to the "Canary" series.)

Type IaB diamonds *do* transmit shortwave ultraviolet light. Diamonds of this type are the rarest of all diamonds and are reportedly being treated with HPHT techniques. This type will not produce colorless or near-colorless stones.

Type II Diamonds

Type IIa and IIb diamonds *do* transmit shortwave ultraviolet light; they cannot absorb it so they *transmit it through the stone.* Type IIa and IIb diamonds *can* be enhanced by HPHT techniques; they can also be *synthetic*:

- *Type IIa diamonds* occur naturally in colorless, near-colorless, brown, and pink shades. In addition, synthetic colorless and near-colorless diamonds are always Type II. Brown-tinted stones of this type can also be transformed into colorless, near-colorless, and fancy pink shades using HPHT techniques. The HPHT treatment removes the brown. As a result, brownish Type IIa diamonds—even those that are extremely tinted—can be transformed into colorless and near-colorless stones. In addition, some brownish diamonds have a pink component that is not visible because the brown tint masks it; in such stones, the HPHT process makes the pink visible by eliminating the brown tint, resulting in a pink diamond. In the same way, naturally pink diamonds with a brownish undertone can be transformed into a purer, more vivid pink. (*Note:* HPHT treatment does not add any pink but simply makes the pink more visible by eliminating the brownish undertone that masks the stone's inherent pink color.)
- *Type IIb diamonds* contain traces of boron and occur naturally in shades of brown or blue. *Synthetic* blue diamonds are also Type IIb. In naturally

occurring diamonds, in rare instances when the boron concentration is extremely low, they may even appear colorless or near-colorless. In addition to the colors they exhibit naturally, the color of Type IIb stones can be enhanced by HPHT techniques. Type IIb diamonds that appear brownish (or near-colorless with a hint of brown) can be transformed by HPHT techniques into *blue* diamonds. Type IIb diamonds that are blue naturally, but exhibit an undesirable brownish undertone, can be transformed into purer, more vivid blues.

When an HPHT enhanced Type IIb diamond becomes blue, its original color was a mixture of blue and brown, but the blue hue was masked by the brown and, thus, diluted or undetectable. Since the HPHT treatment removes the brown color, the result is a much purer, more desirable blue. As was the case with the pink Type IIa diamonds described above, the HPHT treatment does not add any color, but simply makes the blue more visible by eliminating the brownish undertone that was masking the stone's inherent blue color. **NOTE: HPHT methods resulting in a blue diamond is extremely rare.**

* Capital letters are used to name aggregates of Type Ia (A and/or B aggregates), small letters for subdivision of Type I and Type II (Type Ia, Type Ib, Type IIa, Type IIb).

In addition, if checking brownish diamonds, if the SSEF Diamond-Type Spotter indicates you have a Type II diamond, you know the color can be improved; then, if you check the stone with the SSEF Blue Diamond Tester (or electrical conductivity meter), and the indicator shows the stone *is* electrically conductive, you'll know you have a Type IIb, which will yield a rare *blue* diamond when HPHT techniques are used to remove the brown (although it is *extremely* rare to find a brown diamond that is Type IIb and would yield a blue diamond)!

NOTE: *All naturally pink* diamonds, whether they are natural, synthetic, or HPHT-treated, will show a green reaction in the spotter. If checking a "pink" diamond and the reaction is *not* green, you have a stone that is *definitely treated,* but by a different process, such as surface coating.

Where colorless, near-colorless, and blue diamonds are concerned, if the stone does *not* transmit shortwave, you know you don't have to worry or send it to a lab. If it *does,* you know immediately that it *could* be a synthetic diamond or one that has been treated by HPHT techniques, and you *must* submit the stone to a major gem-testing laboratory to know for sure.

Without this handy spotter, everyone without gemological expertise would need to send virtually *every* stone to a lab. Since this is not practical, this simple tool provides a great service by letting you know when a laboratory is needed and when it is not. For gemologists, it is also an invaluable timesaver, because the diamond can be categorized much more quickly by using this tool rather than a microscope.

The spotter will not indicate whether or not you have a Type IaAB diamond, on which HPHT techniques are also being used, but HPHT-treated diamonds of this type will not be colorless, near-colorless, pink, or blue.

HOW TO USE THE SPOTTER

Make sure you have a *shortwave* ultraviolet lamp to use in conjunction with the SSEF Diamond-Type Spotter. The shortwave output from a standard ultraviolet lamp (be sure it provides both longwave and shortwave) including portable models. We use a portable model most of the time because it is easier to control the direction of the shortwave output and can be used with very large diamonds mounted in jewelry. However, for anyone who expects to make frequent use of the spotter to test loose diamonds, we recommend the SSEF Shortwave Illuminator because it is the most powerful shortwave UV light source available for gemological purposes, and it protects against harmful shortwave rays. *WARNING:* USE CAUTION WHEN USING SHORTWAVE: PROTECT YOUR EYES AND SKIN FROM EXPOSURE TO SHORTWAVE AND **NEVER** LOOK INTO THE LAMP. BE SURE THE LIGHT IS DIRECTED AWAY FROM YOUR EYES OR SKIN! With a portable UV lamp, be sure the spotter is placed on a dark, non-reflective surface to prevent reflection of shortwave radiation from the surface toward the user's eyes. For additional eye protection, UV-protective glasses and goggles are available. We recommend using them when working with shortwave ultraviolet.

Be sure to use the spotter in a dark environment (turn off lights or use an ultraviolet viewing cabinet).

IMPORTANT: DO NOT TOUCH THE SMALL WHITE SCREEN BENEATH THE OPENING AT THE TOP OF THE SPOTTER. The screen has been coated with a powdery substance. Touching it, or inadvertently scratching it with tweezers, will destroy it and render the spotter unworkable.

To use the spotter, you simply place the diamond over the opening at the top (see below for directions on how to position the diamond), insert the spotter into the shortwave illuminator, and observe the white-coated area to see whether it fluoresces when you turn on the shortwave lamp. If using a hand-held shortwave ultraviolet lamp, hold the lamp over the stone, turn on the lamp, and note whether or not the coating fluoresces. IMPORTANT NOTE: When using a hand-held ultraviolet lamp, be sure the spotter is placed on a dark surface to prevent shortwave radiation from being reflected from a light colored surface back toward the user's eyes.

Here's how to use it correctly:

1. Remove the cover of the spotter by twisting it gently and pulling up. Before testing a diamond, observe what happens when you turn on the ultraviolet lamp, without a diamond. Notice that at the opening at the top, there is a ring of blue tack (plasticine, also called silly putty) encircling the round opening; lined up directly beneath the opening at the top of the spotter you will see a white screen. The white screen beneath the opening has

been coated with a special substance that fluoresces green when exposed to shortwave ultraviolet light. Before testing your first stone, hold your shortwave UV lamp over the round opening at the top, turn it on, and note the color of the "white" surface—it glows green. The shortwave UV light passes through the open hole and strikes the white background, triggering the green fluorescent response. (If using the SSEF Illuminator, just turn the spotter upside down, insert it into the opening on top of the illuminator, press the button to turn on the shortwave illumination, and look at the specially-coated area of the spotter; it now glows green.)

2. Place the diamond over the opening, positioning it properly. Ideally, the stone should be placed on its side over the opening so that light is transmitted through the girdle of the stone (with the girdle perpendicular to the opening). If this isn't possible, place the stone over the opening with the table-facet facing down and the pavilion pointing up into the air. Make sure you **do not** place the diamond in a face-up position with the pavilion pointing down into the opening.

3. Mold the blue tack carefully around the stone to create a tight seal. This is very important to avoid leakage of the UV light through any opening or gap that might exist alongside the stone. Leakage creates a false green reaction resulting from UV light passing around the stone rather than having been transmitted through it. When the seal is tight, turn on the UV lamp and check the color of the coated white surface under the opening on which the diamond is resting. If using a hand-held shortwave lamp, be sure to hold the lamp away from the front edge of the spotter so that you avoid any spillover of shortwave onto the coated white surface from the front of the unit. This would also create a false reaction simply because you held the lamp too far forward.

4. Check the white screen. Does it remain white, or is it now green? If it is white, you have a diamond that does not transmit shortwave, and you don't have to be concerned about whether or not the color is natural. If it is green, you know that you need a lab to do further testing. The stone may be natural, but it may also be HPHT-treated.

All colorless and near-colorless HPHT-processed diamonds are in the category of diamond types that do transmit shortwave. Most of them are reported to be Type IIa stones, which account for less than 2% of all diamonds. Keep in mind, however, that Type IIa diamonds account for a disproportionately high percentage of large diamonds—over three carats—with high clarity. This means the percentage of treated stones among larger diamonds with high clarity grades may be significantly higher than 2%. Also, keep in mind that all natural-color pink (Type IIa) and most blue (Type IIb) diamonds are extremely rare and valuable, and both natural-color and HPHT-treated stones will transmit shortwave. So it is imperative to confirm whether or not the color is natural when considering any pink diamond and most blue diamonds.

THE SSEF BLUE DIAMOND TESTER

The SSEF Blue Diamond Tester can be invaluable when testing "blue" diamonds as well as brown or brown-tinted diamonds. Natural diamonds that have been treated by radiation techniques, or by surface coating techniques, can be quickly  separated from those with natural color. Natural-color blue diamonds (except the very rare Australian blue-gray/violet blue diamonds, which we've already discussed) obtain their color from the presence of boron, and all boron-containing diamonds are *electro-conductive* (capable of passing an electrical current when a voltage is applied). This is not the case with blue diamonds that have been transformed into blue by irradiation or coating techniques. *So by using the SSEF Blue Diamond Tester—which indicates whether or not the diamond is electro-conductive—one can quickly and easily separate the natural-color from those that have been treated by irradiation or surface coatings.* (Note: it will *not* separate natural blue diamonds from *synthetic* blue diamonds, which also contain boron, but other tests such as fluorescence and phosphorescence can make this distinction). *If the needle on the tester does **not** move (see instructions below), this is positive confirmation of artificial color.* If the needle does move, you know it is electro-conductive and contains boron, so it may be a natural blue diamond, a blue synthetic diamond, or an HPHT-altered blue diamond. Fluorescence will separate the natural from the synthetic blue diamond, but if a natural diamond, you'll need a major lab to determine whether or not the diamond has been subjected to HPHT treatment.

The SSEF Blue Diamond Tester also provides a very useful tool that shows whether HPHT methods can produce a *blue* diamond from one that appears *brown*. HPHT techniques can remove, to varying degrees, the brown tint from Type II diamonds. When the brown is removed, Type IIa diamonds may become colorless, or, in rare cases, pink. Unfortunately, with Type IIa diamonds, there is no way to know which color will be seen following the HPHT treatment until after the treatment. But just the reverse is true with Type IIb diamonds; all Type IIb diamonds contain boron, and therefore, if you know in advance that the stone is IIb, you know even before the HPHT treatment that the resulting color will be some shade of blue!

Type II diamonds—both IIa and IIb—transmit shortwave radiation that can be easily determined using the SSEF Diamond-Type Spotter as described above. But when looking at brown diamonds, knowing whether it is Type IIa or IIb can be invaluable. For this, you must now use the blue diamond tester. We know that Type IIb diamonds contain boron, but, more importantly, they are also *electro-conductive* as mentioned above. So if we can determine whether or not the Type II diamond in question is electro-conductive, we will know whether or not it is IIa or IIb. If the diamond is electrically conductive, you know you have the rare Type IIb, and that when the brown is removed, the color of the diamond *will* be **blue**.

So the SSEF Blue Diamond Tester, used in conjunction with the SSEF Diamond-Type Spotter, is especially valuable in testing brown diamonds and blue diamonds. The SSEF Diamond-Type Spotter will tell you when you have a Type II diamond, and, if so, the blue diamond tester will separate Type IIa from IIb!

The SSEF Blue Diamond Tester is easy to use. It is a simple, portable, battery-operated electrical conductivity meter. As you look at the instrument, you'll notice there is a probe that resembles a pen situated along the right side of the unit. There is a gauge, with a needle that indicates varying degrees of electrical conductivity, beneath which is a dial that can be turned clockwise or counter-clockwise (this can provide an indication of the stone's electro-conductive strength, which could indicate how blue the stone may become). There is also a metal stone-holder for use with unmounted stones (the diamond being tested must be in contact with metal). The tip of the probe has been carefully inserted into a protective casing; to remove it, gently pull the probe toward the lower end of the instrument (and be sure to re-insert it for protection when you have finished testing the diamond). Turn the dial beneath the gauge in the clockwise direction, as far as it will go. Now, take the diamond in question and press the tip of the probe against its table facet (if unmounted, be sure the stone is placed on the metal stone holder in order to establish an electrical circuit). Note whether or not the needle moves. If the needle *moves*, the stone *is electrically conductive;* if it does not move, it is not electrically conductive. If the tester indicates the diamond is electrically conductive, you know you have a Type IIb, and that the color of the diamond following HPHT treatment will be some shade of blue. To determine how electro-conductive it is, and how "blue" the stone might become, turn the dial beneath the gauge slowly counter-clockwise and test again, and repeat this process until the needle stops moving—if the needle still moves when the dial has been turned all the way to the counter-clockwise position, this tells you the stone has significant electro-conductivity and should produce a stronger blue color.

SUMMARY

In summary, when checking *colorless* and *near-colorless* diamonds with the spotter, *no* green reaction with the spotter means it is *not synthetic* and it is *not HPHT-treated.* A green reaction indicates the diamond is a type that *might be synthetic or HPHT-treated* and *requires laboratory verification.*

Remember: *All naturally pink* diamonds, whether they are natural, synthetic, or HPHT-treated, will show a green reaction in the spotter. If checking a "pink" diamond and the reaction is *not* green, you have a stone that is *definitely treated,* but by a different process such as surface coating. The spotter is not useful for fancy-color yellow or greenish yellow diamonds. All diamonds in these colors must be sent to a lab for confirmation, or be accompanied by a current laboratory report. Given the fact that all synthetic colorless diamonds, and those that can be transformed into colorless/near-colorless, stones are Type II, and the fact that Type II diamonds are so rare, the spotter will usually provide reassurance that the stone is natural and its color is natural! So with it, your anxiety, as well as your dependence on laboratories, will be greatly reduced. *NOTE:* MAKE SURE THE STONE YOU ARE TESTING IS A DIAMOND. Natural colorless corundum (sapphire) will *not* transmit short-wave (same reaction with spotter as Type IaA, IaA/B, Ib), but Verneuil synthetics *do* transmit (same reaction with spotter as Type IIa, IIb, IaB).

If you know a stone is sapphire, but aren't sure if it is natural or synthetic, the spotter can be used to distinguish between the two!

Diamond Reactions to the SSEF Diamond-Type Spotter

Diamond Color	NATURAL COLOR DIAMONDS		HPHT-TREATED DIAMONDS	
	Diamond Type	Spotter Reaction	Diamond Type	Spotter Reaction
Colorless* (D–Z color, not *fancy* color)	Most are Ia	No green	Ia—tinted stones transformed into various fancy-colors	No Green
	Type IIa (very rare)	Green**	IIa—tinted stones transformed into colorless	Green**
Pink	Type IIa	Green**	IIa—tinted stones transformed into pink or into purer, more vivid pink	Green**
Blue	Most are IIb	Green**	IIb—tinted stones transformed into blue or into purer, more vivid blue	Green**
	Ia (hydrogen present—very rare)	No green		

*All colorless synthetic diamonds now in the marketplace are type IIa and will give a green reaction with the spotter.

**Further testing is required at a major gem testing laboratory.

About the "RIGHT-WAY" Series on Using Gem Identification Tools

The Antoinette Matlins "RIGHT-WAY" Series is a set of essential booklets that explains in non-technical terms how to use individual gem identification instruments to identify diamonds and colored gems, and how to separate natural gems from imitations, treated gemstones, synthetics, and look-alikes. The approach is direct and practical, and its style is easy to understand. In fact, with these highly accessible guide booklets, anyone can begin to master gem identification. The booklet series is based on the bestselling book *Gem Identification Made Easy: A Hands-On Guide to More Confident Buying & Selling* (5th Edition) by Antoinette Matlins, PG, FGA, and A. C. Bonanno, FGA, ASA, MGA.

Using a simple, step-by-step system developed by the authors, the series explains how to properly use essential but uncomplicated instruments to identify gems by explaining what to look for gemstone by gemstone. The key to avoiding costly mistakes and recognizing profitable opportunities is knowing both what to look for and what to look out for. In total, it is a basic introduction to gem identification that will enable anyone interested in gems to understand how to identify them.

THE CONCEPTS

Each booklet in the series explores one or more gem identification instruments, and provides an overview of when and why to use them, step-by-step instructions on how to use each, and what will be shown—or not be shown. It guides the reader on using each instrument with any precious gemstones they are trying to identify.

Chelsea and Synthetic
Emerald Filters Made Easy
978-0-9904152-0-6

Dichroscopes Made Easy
978-0-9904152-1-3

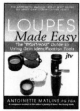

Loupes Made Easy
978-0-9904152-2-0

Refractometers Made Easy
978-0-9904152-0-6

SSEF Diamond-Type Spotter and
Blue Diamond Tester Made Easy
978-0-9904152-5-1

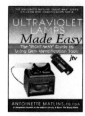

Ultraviolet Lamps
Made Easy
978-0-9904152-4-4

Antoinette Matlins, PG, FGA, is an internationally respected gem and jewelry expert, author and lecturer. Honored with the international Accredited Gemologists Association's highest award for excellence in gemology, Ms. Matlins's books are published in seven languages and are widely used throughout the world by consumers and professionals in the gem and jewelry field. Her books include *Gem Identification Made Easy: A Hands-On Guide to More Confident Buying & Selling; Jewelry & Gems: The Buying Guide* (over 400,000 copies now in print—the only book of its kind ever offered by *Consumer Reports*); and *Jewelry & Gems at Auction: The Definitive Guide to Buying & Selling at the Auction House & on Internet Auction Sites* (all from GemStone Press).

Former gemology editor of *National Jeweler* magazine, her articles and comments on buying and selling gems and jewelry and on gem investment have appeared in many national and international consumer and trade publications. She is also the author of the "Gemstones" chapter in the *Encyclopedia of Investments,* 2nd Edition.

Ms. Matlins has gained wide recognition as a dedicated consumer advocate. She has spearheaded the Accredited Gemologists Association's nationwide campaign against gemstone investment telemarketing scams. A popular media guest, she has been seen on ABC, CBS, NBC and CNN educating consumers about gems and jewelry and exposing fraud.

In addition to her educational work, Ms. Matlins is retained by clients worldwide to seek fine, rare or unusual gems and jewels for acquisition.

For more information on seminars and workshops given by Antoinette Matlins, visit www.gemstonepress.com.

OTHER BOOKS BY ANTOINETTE MATLINS

Colored Gemstones: The Antoinette Matlins Buying Guide

Diamonds: The Antoinette Matlins Buying Guide

Engagement & Wedding Rings: The Definitive Buying Guide for People in Love

Gem Identification Made Easy: A Hands-On Guide to More Confident Buying & Selling

Jewelry & Gems at Auction: The Definitive Guide to Buying & Selling at the Auction House & on Internet Auction Sites

Jewelry & Gems: The Buying Guide

The Pearl Book: The Definitive Buying Guide

GemStone Press

Helping to increase understanding, appreciation and enjoyment of jewelry, gems and gemology.

GemStone Press is an international source for books, gem-identification equipment and other items designed to help consumers and people in the gem trade learn more about jewelry, gems and gemology.

GemStone Press books are easy to read, easy to use. They are designed for the person who does not have a scientific or technical background.

Visit www.gemstonepress.com/category/GII.html for more information on our extensive selection of gem identification equipment. All gem identification equipment we supply has been tested and chosen by Antoinette Matlins for its quality.

GemStone Press
Sunset Farm Offices, Route 4
P.O. Box 237 • Woodstock, VT 05091
Tel (802) 457-4000   Fax (802) 457-4004
Orders: (800) 962-4544 (8:30AM–5:30PM ET Mon.–Fri.)
www.gemstonepress.com

CPSIA information can be obtained at www.ICGtesting.com
Printed in the USA
BVOW03s0558280714

360452BV00002B/74/P

9 780990 415251